AMAZING SUPER SIMPLE INVENTIONS

SUPER SIMPLE

PHONOGRAPH

PROJECTS

INSPIRING & EDUCATIONAL
SCIENCE ACTIVITIES

ALEX KUSKOWSKI

Consulting Editor, Diane Craig, M.A./Reading Specialist

Super Sandcastle

An Imprint of Abdo Publishing
abdopublishing.com

abdopublishing.com

Published by Abdo Publishing, a division of ABDO, PO Box 398166, Minneapolis, Minnesota 55439. Copyright © 2016 by Abdo Consulting Group, Inc. International copyrights reserved in all countries. No part of this book may be reproduced in any form without written permission from the publisher. Super SandCastle™ is a trademark and logo of Abdo Publishing.

Printed in the United States of America, North Mankato, Minnesota
062015
092015

Editor: Liz Salzmann
Content Developer: Nancy Tuminelly
Cover and Interior Design and Production: Mighty Media, Inc.
Photo Credits: Library of Congress, Mighty Media, Inc., Shutterstock, Wikicommons

Library of Congress Cataloging-in-Publication Data

Kuskowski, Alex.
 Super simple phonograph projects : inspiring & educational science activities / Alex Kuskowski ; consulting editor, Diane Craig, M.A./Reading Specialist.
     pages cm. -- (Amazing super simple inventions)
  ISBN 978-1-62403-731-3
 1. Sounds--Experiments--Juvenile literature. 2. Sound-waves--Experiments--Juvenile literature. 3. Phonograph--Juvenile literature. I. Title.
  QC225.5.K87 2016
  621.389'32--dc23
                    2014049932

Super SandCastle™ books are created by a team of professional educators, reading specialists, and content developers around five essential components—phonemic awareness, phonics, vocabulary, text comprehension, and fluency—to assist young readers as they develop reading skills and strategies and increase their general knowledge. All books are written, reviewed, and leveled for guided reading and early reading intervention programs for use in shared, guided, and independent reading and writing activities to support a balanced approach to literacy instruction.

To Adult Helpers

The projects in this title are fun and simple. There are just a few things to remember to keep kids safe. Some projects require the use of sharp or hot objects. Also, kids may be using messy materials such as glue. Make sure they protect their clothes and work surfaces. Review the projects before starting, and be ready to assist when necessary.

KEY SYMBOLS

Watch for these warning symbols in this book. Here is what they mean.

HOT!
You will be working with something hot. Get help!

SHARP!
You will be working with a sharp object. Get help!

CONTENTS

PHONOGRAPHS

AN INTRODUCTION

Have you heard of the phonograph? It was an important invention. It was the first machine that could record sound and play it back.

Thomas Edison invented many things, from the lightbulb to the first movie. The phonograph was one of his most famous inventions. Learn how the phonograph works. Do experiments. Discover the invention of recorded sound for yourself!

PARTS OF A PHONOGRAPH

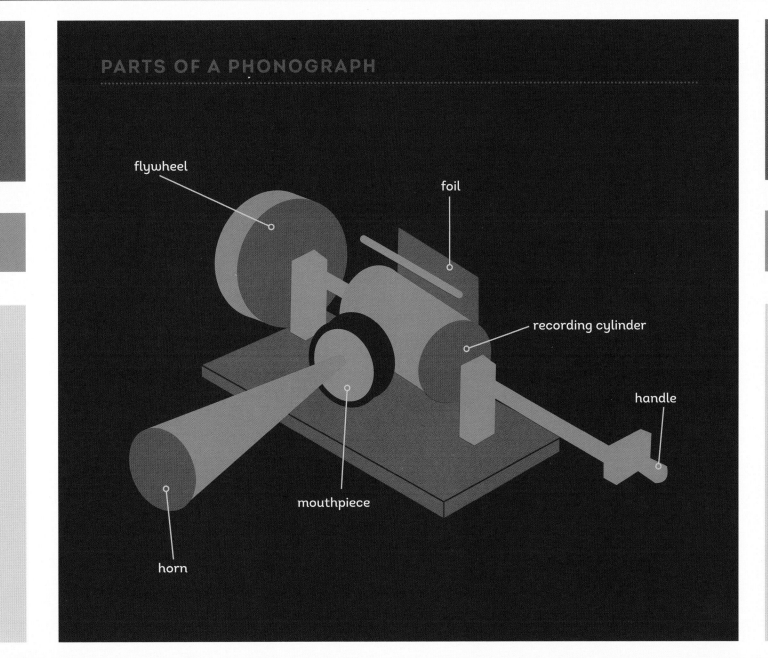

flywheel

foil

recording cylinder

handle

mouthpiece

horn

THOMAS EDISON

Before Thomas Alva Edison became famous, he was a scientist who experimented at home.

The invention that made Edison famous was the phonograph. It was the first machine to record and play back sound!

People called Edison the Wizard of Menlo Park. They thought the phonograph was magical! People used phonographs to listen to music for more than a hundred years. The phonograph was Edison's favorite invention!

OTHER IMPORTANT PEOPLE

ÉDOUARD-LÉON SCOTT DE MARTINVILLE

He invented a machine that made pictures of sound that could be read.

ALEXANDER GRAHAM BELL

He made the phonograph sound better by using wax to record the sound.

EMILE BERLINER

He improved the phonograph. He recorded on flat discs. We still use flat records today.

THEN TO NOW

A TIMELINE OF THE PHONOGRAPH

Édouard-Léon Scott de Martinville invented the phonautograph. It made pictures of sounds for people to read.

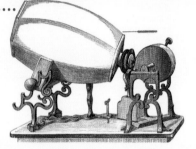

Alexander Graham Bell improved Edison's phonograph. He named it the Graphophone.

1857　　**1877**　　**1881**　　**1888**

Thomas Edison invented the phonograph.

Emile Berliner improved the phonograph further. His invention used a flat surface to play and record music instead of a **cylinder**.

Orlando R. Marsh started making records electrically with **microphones**.

Today there are **CDs** and **MP3s**. But some people still use phonographs!

1901   **1924**   **1950s**   **TODAY**

The Victor Talking Machine Company sold Victrolas. They were the most popular brand of phonograph.

33⅓ **rpm** and 45 rpm records became the standard record sizes.

BE AN INVENTOR

LEARN HOW TO THINK LIKE AN INVENTOR!

Inventors have a special way of working. It is a series of steps called the Scientific Method. Follow the steps to work like an inventor.

THE SCIENTIFIC METHOD

1. QUESTION

What question are you trying to answer? Write down the question.

2. GUESS

Try to guess the answer to your question. Write down your guess.

3. EXPERIMENT

Think of a way to find the answer. Write down the steps.

KEEP TRACK

There's another way to be just like an inventor. Inventors make notes about everything they do. So get a notebook. When you do an experiment, write down what happens in each step. It's super simple!

4. MATERIALS

What supplies will you need? Make a list.

5. ANALYSIS

Do the experiment. What happened? Write down the results.

6. CONCLUSION

Was your guess correct? Why or why not?

MATERIALS

33⅓ rpm record

balloons

can opener

cardboard

clear tape

compass

duct tape

flat gems

glue gun & glue sticks

laser pointer

marker

pencil

Here are some of the **materials** that you will need.

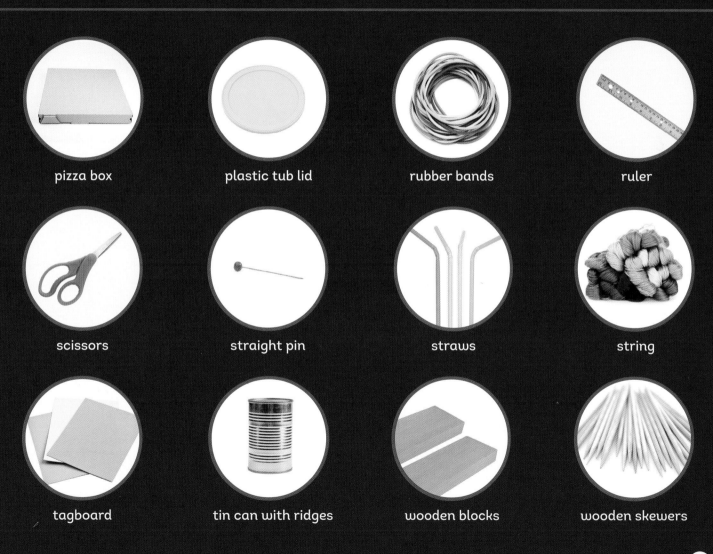

pizza box

plastic tub lid

rubber bands

ruler

scissors

straight pin

straws

string

tagboard

tin can with ridges

wooden blocks

wooden skewers

SOUND SECRETS

Discover where sound comes from!

MATERIALS: empty tin can with ridges, can opener, scissors, balloon, rubber band, wooden skewer

When something **vibrates**, it creates a sound. The vibrations are called sound waves. The sound waves carry the sound to your ears.

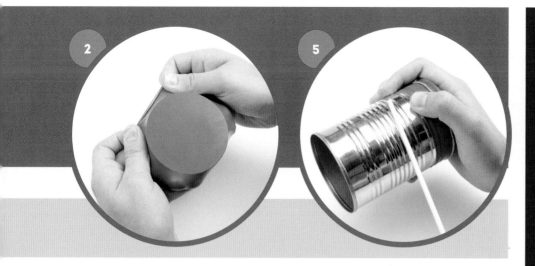

MAKE A SECRET SOUND

① Use the can opener to remove the bottom of the can.

② Cut off the bottom of the balloon. Stretch the top of the balloon over one end of the can.

③ Hold the balloon in place with a rubber band.

④ Run the skewer along the can. Listen to the sound.

⑤ Put your hand over the balloon. Run the skewer along the can again. Does it sound the same?

HOW DOES IT WORK?

A phonograph needle runs over bumps on a record. The bumps make the needle **vibrate**. This causes sound waves. The skewer going over the bumps on the can made sound waves.

CONE PROJECTOR

Find out the secrets of sound!

MATERIALS: string, ruler, scissors, pencil, tagboard, clear tape

Sound waves **bounce** off of things. When the sound waves bounce off of a cone shape, they get louder.

HOW DOES IT WORK?

When you yell, the sound goes freely in all directions. The cone makes the sound waves bounce around. It also points the sound in a certain direction. The sound gets louder.

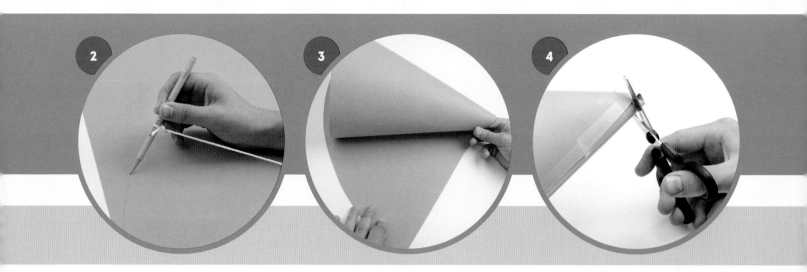

MAKE A CONE PROJECTOR

① Cut a string 12 inches (31 cm) long. Tie one end around a pencil. Lay the tagboard down **horizontally**.

② Hold the pencil near the bottom left corner. Pull the string to the middle of the bottom edge of the tagboard.

Hold it there. Move the pencil to draw a half circle on the tagboard. Cut out the shape.

③ Roll the tagboard into a cone. Tape the edge.

④ Cut ½ inch (1.3 cm) off the point of the cone.

⑤ Yell as loud as you can. Then put the point of the cone to your mouth. Yell as loud as you can through the cone.

SEE SOUND WAVES

Sound off and watch the waves move!

MATERIALS: empty tin can, can opener, balloon, scissors, rubber band, large flat gem, craft glue, paper, ruler, double-sided tape, 2 wooden blocks, laser pointer

Sound is made of waves. Sound waves can make things move.

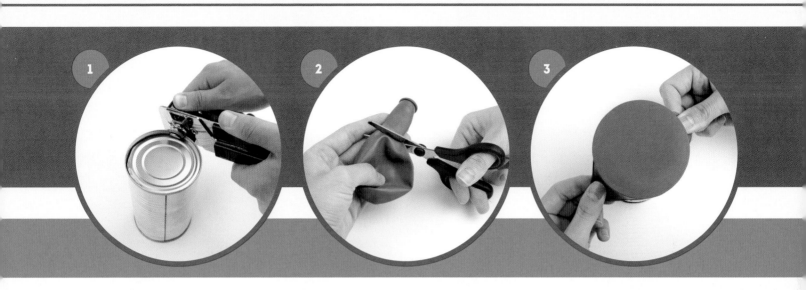

MAKE SOUND WAVES

1. Remove the bottom of the can.

2. Cut off the bottom of the balloon.

3. Stretch the top of the balloon over one end of the can.

4. Hold the balloon in place with a rubber band.

continued on next page

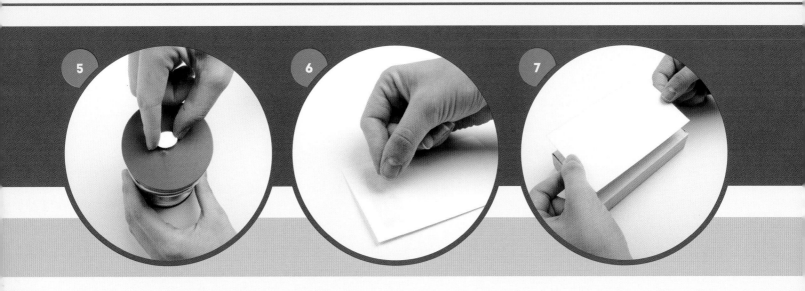

MAKE SOUND WAVES (CONTINUED)

5 Glue a large gem to the center of the balloon. Face the colored side toward the balloon.

6 Cut a rectangle out of paper. Make it the same size as the wooden blocks. Put double-sided tape on one side of the rectangle.

7 Tape the rectangle to a wooden block.

8 Set the block on a short end. Put the other block 12 inches (31 cm) away. Set it on a long side.

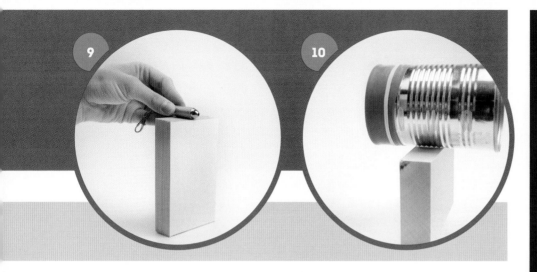

9 Put the laser pointer on top of the taller block.

10 Put the can on the shorter block. Face the gem toward the laser pointer.

11 Have a friend shine the laser pointer at the gem. Make sure the light reflects onto the paper on the tall block.

12 Yell into the can. Watch the light on the paper!

HOW DOES IT WORK?

The gem moves when sound waves hit the balloon. That makes the light move. It shows the sound waves on the paper rectangle.

VOICE RECORDER

Picture the sound of your voice!

MATERIALS: empty tin can, can opener, scissors, balloon, rubber band, compass, paper, cardboard, scissors, pencil, straw, masking tape, wooden block, marker, clear tape

Edison's phonograph was wonderful. It not only played sounds, but it could record sounds too. Make your own sound recorder.

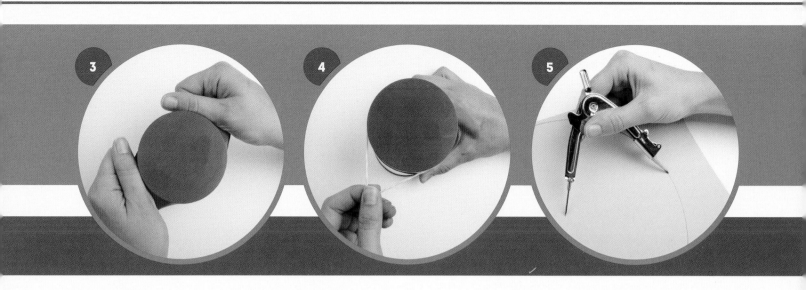

MAKE A VOICE RECORDER

① Remove the bottom of the can.

② Cut off the bottom of the balloon.

③ Stretch the top of the balloon over one end of the can.

④ Hold the balloon in place with a rubber band.

⑤ Draw a 9-inch (23 cm) circle on paper.

⑥ Draw the same size circle on cardboard. Cut the circles out.

continued on next page

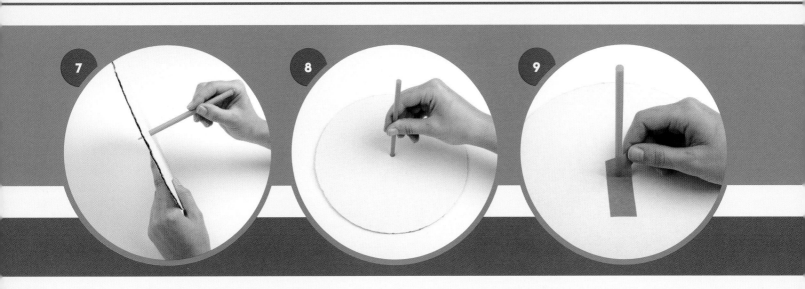

MAKE A VOICE RECORDER (CONTINUED)

7 Use a pencil to poke a hole in the center of the circles.

8 Put a straw through the hole in the cardboard circle.

9 Set the cardboard circle down. Tape the cardboard circle to the straw.

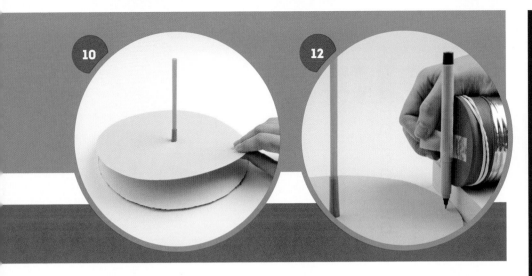

10 Put the paper circle on top of the cardboard circle.

11 Set the block against the circle. Set the can on top of the block. Face the balloon toward the circle.

12 Hold the marker against the balloon. The point of the marker should touch the paper. Tape the marker in place.

13 Have a friend slowly turn the straw. The marker should make a light mark on the paper as it spins. Speak loudly into the can.

HOW DOES IT WORK?

When the circle turns, the marker makes a line on the paper. Sound waves from your voice make the marker move. The line changes. This is a very simple example of a recording phonograph.

PHONOGRAPH

Make your own record player!

MATERIALS: 2 pencils, pizza box, small plastic tub lid, 33⅓ rpm record, duct tape, string, ruler, tagboard, scissors, straight pin, hot glue gun & glue sticks, cardboard

Phonograph records are made of **vinyl**. The recording machine makes **grooves** in the vinyl. When a phonograph needle runs in the grooves, the music comes alive!

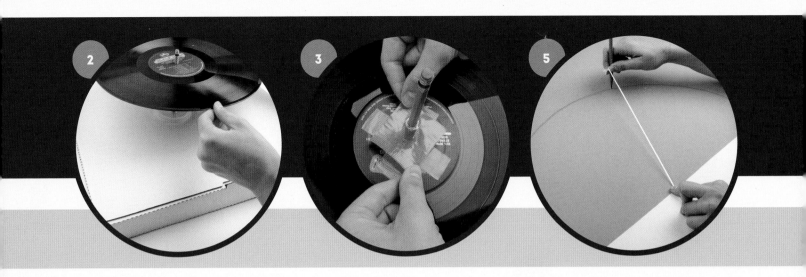

MAKE A PHONOGRAPH

① Use a pencil to make a hole in the center of the pizza box. Then use the pencil to make a hole in the center of the plastic lid.

② Lay the lid face up on the pizza box. Push the pencil through both holes. Put the record on the pencil.

③ Tape the record to the pencil. Use several pieces of tape. Make sure it is secure.

④ Cut a string 12 inches (31 cm) long. Tie one end around the second pencil. Lay the tagboard down **horizontally**.

⑤ Hold the pencil near the bottom left corner. Pull the string to the middle of the bottom edge of the tagboard. Hold it there. Move the pencil to draw a half circle on the tagboard. Cut out the shape.

continued on next page

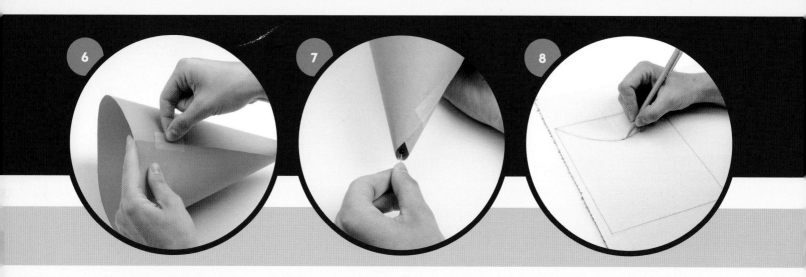

MAKE A PHONOGRAPH (CONTINUED)

6 Roll the tagboard into a cone. Leave an opening at the small end. Tape the edge.

7 Hot glue the pin inside the small end of the cone. The point should be sticking out of the cone.

8 Draw a rectangle on cardboard. Make it 6 inches (15 cm) by 8 inches (20 cm). Draw a dot 2 inches (5 cm) from the center of a short side.

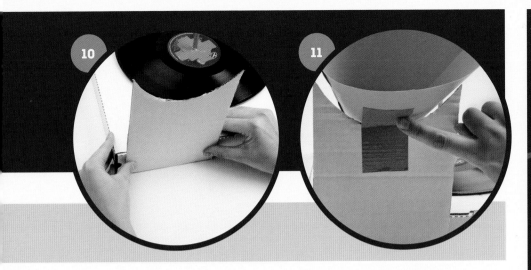

⑨ Draw a half circle from the dot to the nearest corners. Cut out the half circle.

⑩ Hot glue the cardboard to the side of the pizza box. Place it ½ inch (1.3 cm) from a corner. Make sure the half circle is pointing up.

⑪ Set the cone in the half circle. Make sure the pin can reach the record. Tape the cone in place.

⑫ Touch the point of the needle to the record. Spin the record slowly.

HOW DOES IT WORK?

The needle runs over the bumps in the **groove**. The bumps make the needle **vibrate**. This makes sound waves. The sound is carried through the cone. You can hear the music play!

CONCLUSION

Music is part of daily life. You can play it on a **CD**, on a computer, or even on a phone. That all started with Edison's phonograph. This book is the first step in discovering the notes of history. There is a lot more to find out.

Learn more about recorded music. Look online or at the library. Think of recording crafts and experiments you can do on your own.

Put on your scientist thinking cap and go on a learning journey!

QUIZ

1. The flywheel is a part of the phonograph. **TRUE OR FALSE?**

2. What was Thomas Edison's nickname?

3. What is another name for the phonograph?

THINK ABOUT IT!

Did the phonograph change how people listened to music? Why or why not?

Answers: 1. True 2. Wizard of Menlo Park 3. Gramophone, talking machine, record player, turntable

GLOSSARY

bounce – to spring up or back after hitting something.

CD – a round, plastic disc that music or computer files can be stored on. *CD* is short for *compact disc*.

cylinder – a solid, round shape with flat ends. A soda can is a cylinder.

groove – a long, narrow crack or rut.

horizontally – with the long edge in the same direction as the ground, or side-to-side.

material – something needed to make or build something else.

microphone – a device that captures sound and sends it to a recorder.

MP3 – a digital sound recording that can be played on a device such as a computer or mobile phone.

rpm – a measurement of how many times something turns all the way around in one minute. It stands for *revolutions per minute*.

vibrate – to make very small, quick movements back and forth.

vinyl – a material used to make things such as record albums, clothes, and floors.